First World War
and Army of Occupation
War Diary
France, Belgium and Germany

1 DIVISION
2 Infantry Brigade
King's (Liverpool Regiment)
9th Battalion
12 March 1915 - 31 December 1915

WO95/1269/3

The Naval & Military Press Ltd
www.nmarchive.com
Published in association with The National Archives

Published by

The Naval & Military Press Ltd

Unit 10 Ridgewood Industrial Park,

Uckfield, East Sussex,

TN22 5QE England

Tel: +44 (0) 1825 749494

www.naval-military-press.com

www.nmarchive.com

This diary has been reprinted in facsimile from the original. Any imperfections are inevitably reproduced and the quality may fall short of modern type and cartographic standards.

© **Crown Copyright**
Images reproduced by permission of The National Archives, London, England, 2015.

Contents

Document type	Place/Title	Date From	Date To
Heading	WO95/1269/3		
Heading	1st Division 2nd Brigade.1-9th Battalion The King's (Liverpool Regt) 1915 Mar-Sept 1915		
Heading	2nd Infantry Brigade. 1st Division. (Arrived France from England 13.3.15. Joined Bde.29.3.15) War Diary 1/9th Battn. The King's (Liverpool Regiment). March 1915		
Heading	On His Majesty's Service.		
Heading	War Diary of 1/9th Battalion The King's (Liverpool Regt) T.F For March 1915		
War Diary	Tunbridge Wells	12/03/1915	12/03/1915
War Diary	Southampton	12/03/1915	12/03/1915
War Diary	Le Havre	13/03/1915	13/03/1915
War Diary	Le Havre	13/03/1915	14/03/1915
War Diary	Le Havre	14/03/1915	14/03/1915
War Diary	Hazebrouck	15/03/1915	15/03/1915
War Diary	Choques	15/03/1915	15/03/1915
War Diary	Oblinghem (Near. Bethune	15/03/1915	15/03/1915
War Diary	Les Facons	24/03/1915	24/03/1915
Heading	2nd Infantry Brigade. 1st Division. War Diary 1/9th Battn. The King's (Liverpool Regiment). April 1915		
Heading	On His Majesty's Service.		
Heading	War Diary of 1/9th Battalion The King's (Liverpool Regt) TF For April 1915		
War Diary	Les Facons Near Bethune	06/04/1915	24/04/1915
War Diary	Richebourg St. Vaast	24/04/1915	28/04/1915
Heading	2nd Infantry Brigade. 1st Division. War Diary. 1/9th Battn. The King's (Liverpool Regiment). May 1915		
Heading	On His Majesty's Service.		
War Diary	Richebourg St Vaast	01/05/1915	01/05/1915
War Diary	Avelette	02/05/1915	02/05/1915
War Diary	Hinges	03/05/1915	05/05/1915
War Diary	Pont Tournant	06/05/1915	06/05/1915
War Diary	Les Chocques	07/05/1915	07/05/1915
War Diary	Richebourg L'Avoue	08/05/1915	09/05/1915
War Diary	Essars	09/05/1915	09/05/1915
War Diary	Lannoy	10/05/1915	11/05/1915
War Diary	Bethune	12/05/1915	12/05/1915
War Diary	Beuvry	15/05/1915	15/05/1915
War Diary	Cambrin	20/05/1915	21/05/1915
War Diary	Annequin	24/05/1915	24/05/1915
War Diary	Cambrin	28/05/1915	28/05/1915
War Diary	Cuinchy	29/05/1915	29/05/1915
Heading	2nd Infantry Brigade. 1st Division. War Diary 1/9th Battn. The King's (Liverpool Regiment). June 1915		
Heading	On His Majesty's Service.		
War Diary	Annequin	01/06/1915	01/06/1915
War Diary	Labeuvriere	04/06/1915	11/06/1915
War Diary	Cuinchy	16/06/1915	18/06/1915
War Diary	Verquin	19/06/1915	19/06/1915

War Diary	Lapugnoy	24/06/1915	26/06/1915
War Diary	Sailly Labourse	27/06/1915	30/06/1915
Heading	2nd Infantry Brigade. 1st Division. War Diary. 1/9th Battn. The King's (Liverpool Regiment). July 1915		
Heading	On His Majesty's Service.		
War Diary	Cambrin	02/07/1915	06/07/1915
War Diary	Sailly Labourse	07/07/1915	09/07/1915
War Diary	Faubourg D'arras Bethune	12/07/1915	12/07/1915
War Diary	Labourse	19/07/1915	24/07/1915
War Diary	Vermelles	25/07/1915	30/07/1915
War Diary	Faubourg D'Arras Bethune	31/07/1915	31/07/1915
Heading	2nd Infantry Brigade. 1st Division. War Diary. 1/9th Battn. The King's (Liverpool Regiment). August 1915		
Heading	On His Majesty's Service.		
War Diary	Faubourg D'Arras Bethune	03/08/1915	06/08/1915
War Diary	Annequin	07/08/1915	15/08/1915
War Diary	Labourse	16/08/1915	16/08/1915
War Diary	Garden City	18/08/1915	23/08/1915
War Diary	Annequin	24/08/1915	27/08/1915
War Diary	Noyelles-Les-Vermelles	28/08/1915	31/08/1915
Heading	2nd Infantry Brigade. 1st Division. War Diary 1/9th Battn. The King's (Liverpool Regiment). September 1915		
War Diary	Noyelles	01/09/1915	03/09/1915
War Diary	Burbure	17/09/1915	30/09/1915
Heading	2nd Infantry Brigade. 1st Division. (Left Bde. to.Join 3rd Bde.12.11.15) War Diary 1/9th Battn. The King's (Liverpool Regiment). October 1915		
Heading	On His Majesty's Service.		
War Diary		01/10/1915	31/10/1915
Heading	1st Division 3rd Brigade.1-9th Battalion The King's (Liverpool Regt.) Nov-Dec 1915		
Heading	2nd Infantry Brigade. 1st Division. (joined Bde. From 2nd Bde. 1st Div.12.11.15) War Diary 1/9th Battn. The King's (Liverpool Regiment). November 1915		
Heading	On His Majesty's Service.		
War Diary	Lillers	01/11/1915	15/11/1915
War Diary	Houchin	19/11/1915	19/11/1915
War Diary	Philosophe	21/11/1915	26/11/1915
War Diary	Loos and Hulluch	28/11/1915	29/11/1915
War Diary	G 23 a	30/11/1915	30/11/1915
Heading	3rd Infantry Brigade. 1st Division War Diary 1/9th Battn. The King's (Liverpool Regiment). December 1915		
Heading	On His Majesty's Service.		
War Diary	G 23	01/12/1915	02/12/1915
War Diary	Noeux Les Mines	03/12/1915	08/12/1915
War Diary	G 17 B-D	09/12/1915	11/12/1915
War Diary	H 19 A to G 18 B	12/12/1915	14/12/1915
War Diary	G 17 B and D	15/12/1915	17/12/1915
War Diary	H 19 A to G 18 B	18/12/1915	20/12/1915
War Diary	Mazingarbe	21/12/1915	26/12/1915
War Diary	H 25 A-H 19 A	27/12/1915	29/12/1915
War Diary	G 23-G 24	30/12/1915	31/12/1915

WO 95/12691(3)

1ST DIVISION
2ND BRIGADE

1-9TH BATTALION
THE KING'S (LIVERPOOL REGT)
1915 MAR - OCT 1915   STET   1915 DEC

To 55 DIV. 166 Bde

2nd Infantry Brigade.

1st Division.

(Arrived France from England
13.3.15. Joined Bde.
29.3.15).

WAR DIARY

1/9th BATTN. THE KING'S (LIVERPOOL REGIMENT).

M A R C H

1 9 1 5

On His Majesty's Service.

CONFIDENTIAL

War Diary.

of

1/9th Battalion The King's (Liverpool Regt) T.F.

For

March. 1915.

March 1915

Army Form C. 2118.

WAR DIARY
or
INTELLIGENCE SUMMARY.

of the 1/9th Battn. The King's (Liverpool Regt) T.F

(Erase heading not required.)

Instructions regarding War Diaries and Intelligence Summaries are contained in F.S. Regs., Part II. and the Staff Manual respectively. Title pages will be prepared in manuscript.

Hour, Date, Place	Summary of Events and Information	Remarks and references to Appendices
Tunbridge Wells March 12th	Battalion entrained (3 trains) for Service Overseas 29 officers 947 N.C.O's men	Aut
Southampton March 12. 5 pm	23 Vehicles 72 horses and mules. New armament with C.L.M.L.E converted to Mark III A with sling Reserve	Aut
	Embarked on "Golden Eagle", "Inventor" + "Duchess of Argyle". (left Q.M. at Hutting Hospital)	Aut
Le Havre March 13 6.40 am	Disembarked and marched to Camp at Sanvic 28 officers + 947 other ranks	Aut
Le Havre March 14 4.0 am	Marched off to Railway Station (Gare des Marchandises) in two platoons	Aut
Le Havre March 14th 9.30 am	Train left for Hazebrouck [via Rouen and Abbeville]	Aut
Hazebrouck March 15th 5.30 am	Train arr'd in to Choques	Aut
Choques March 15 6.30	Disentrained at Choques and marched to Billets at Oblinghem	Aut
Oblinghem (near Bethune)	Sent available officers and men for instruction in trench duties and armament exercises. Attached to 3rd Brigade for training, administration	Aut
March 24th 3.0 pm	Bn. attached to 1st Brigade for Working off	Aut
	Moved out of Oblinghem 28 officers 926 N.C.O's + men	Aut
Les Facons March 24	Now in Billets with H.Q. at Mesplaux	Aut
March 27	Two first line & B reinforcements from B.E.F arrive 2 officers 82 O.R.	for Aut
28	3rd line reinforcement from the King's Liverpool Regiment Port Sunlight arrives	for Aut

Theo J Rolland
Major, Commanding
1/9th Battn. The King's
(Liverpool Regt) T.F

2nd Infantry Brigade.
1st Division.

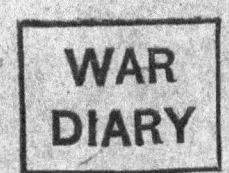

1/9th BATTN. THE KING'S (LIVERPOOL REGIMENT).

A P R I L

1 9 1 5

On His Majesty's Service.

CONFIDENTIAL

War Diary

of

1/9th Battalion The King's (Liverpool Regt) T.F.

For

April 1915

Army Form C. 2118.

April 1915

WAR DIARY
or
INTELLIGENCE SUMMARY.
(Erase heading not required.)

of the 1/9th Battn The King's (Liverpool Regt) T.F.

Instructions regarding War Diaries and Intelligence Summaries are contained in F.S. Regs., Part II. and the Staff Manual respectively. Title pages will be prepared in manuscript.

Hour, Date, Place	Summary of Events and Information	Remarks and references to Appendices
LES FACONS nr BETHUNE April 6th	A and B companies went into the trenches by platoons with the 2nd Royal Sussex and 1st Northampton, respectively at Neuve Chapelle	Aut
April 9th	One man wounded (since died). A Coy and Batt caps came out on 15th. C + D companies went into the trenches by platoons with the	Aut
	2nd Royal Sussex and 1st Northampton respectively.	Aut
April 12 5.30 am	C coy had 3 men wounded. D Coy one man wounded since died	Aut
April 12 8.0 pm	Company came out of the trenches.	Aut
April 13 2.0 pm	A, B + C coys marched to Billets in ORLINGHEM	Aut
April 13	D. Coys marched to Billets in ORLINGHEM	Aut
" 16th	Lieut Workman R.A.M.C attached to unit in place of Major Mahony R.A.M.C invalided.	Aut
" 18	2nd Lieut BOBBITT + 2nd Lieut PARKER joined for duty from 2nd Battalion	Aut
April 24	2nd Lieuts NOTT, RUSSELL & COOTE gazetted to Battalion.	Aut
	Battalion has A + B coys and number of Scottish marched 15 miles in	Aut
RICHEBOURG ST VAAST	A. and 1 miles 2" K.R.R. to trenches in Sector D.2. (3 wounded)	Aut
April 28 6.15 P	B " 1/B.W Northampts to trenches in Sector D.3. (3 Killed)	Aut
	C + D coys both the places of A + B cy M gun. remained in	Aut
	C. coy had 2 wounded. D coy. 1 killed and 3 wounded	Aut

Theo J Bollard
Major Commanding
1/9th Batt The King's (Liverpool Regt) T.F.

2nd Infantry Brigade.
1st Division.

WAR DIARY

1/9th BATTN. THE KING'S (LIVERPOOL REGIMENT).

M A Y

1 9 1 5

On His Majesty's Service.

Army Form C. 2118.

1/9th Battn "The King's"
(Liverpool Regt.) 78° MAY 1915

WAR DIARY
or
INTELLIGENCE SUMMARY.
(Erase heading not required.)

Instructions regarding War Diaries and Intelligence Summaries are contained in F.S. Regs., Part II. and the Staff Manual respectively. Title pages will be prepared in manuscript.

Commanding 1/9th Battn "THE KING'S"
Lieut. Col.

Hour, Date, Place	Summary of Events and Information	Remarks and references to Appendices
1915		
May 1. RICHEBOURG S-VAAST	One other rank killed and one wounded	
4.30 p 2. AVELETTE	Battalion less C and D Companies marched to AVELETTE, C and D Companies followed later on being relieved in Trenches	
5 p.m 3. HINGES	Battalion marched by Bus to HINGES	
2 pm 6. PONT TOURNANT	Battalion marched to PONT TOURNANT and bivouacked	
10 pm 7. LES GLORIEUX	Battalion marched to LES CHOQUES	
6 pm 8. RICHEBOURG L'AVOUE	Battalion moved into Battle Positions in Sub/section D2 at RUE DU BOIS	
9. "	Transport to MESPLEUX...	
	Attack by 2nd Infantry Brigade — Battalion moved into 3rd line Trenches & 2nd Brigade moved out of front line. 6 am to support...	
	2.1 K.R.R. Battalion ordered to 11.15 am to move forward...	
	4.12.40 pm attacked...	
	4.1.45 pm... at 1.45 pm Battn...	
	to 1st Army Reserve... A and C...	
	Coys moved to Support. 7.45 pm B...	
	Battalion at...	
6.30 p 9. ESSARS	1st Coldstream Guards... LE TOURET to ESSARS.	
	Casualties 57. 3 killed (Major T.T. Rolland & 2/Lt SEPTIMUS)	
	Wounded (Lt Col A.W. FULTON, Lt & Adj D. Diggory, 2/Lts E BAYNE)	
	Other Ranks No. 12 killed. 66 wounded. 2 missing, Shell shock 2	
7.15 pm 10. LANNOY	Battalion to ESSARS per Lannoy	
11.0 11.	Coys to BETHUNE	
3.0 pm 12. BETHUNE	Battalion marched to BETHUNE	
12.0 15. BEUVRY	Battalion marched to BEUVRY	
2.30 p 20. CAMBRIN	Battalion marched to CAMBRIN and relieved R.WELSH FUSILIERS	
21.	1 Company (R Welch Regt) on 21.5...	
	Casualties 1 other rank killed 7 wounded	
2.30 p 24. ANNEQUIN	Battalion relieved by 1/LN LANCS. marched to ANNEQUIN, Brigade Reserve	
25. CAMBRIN	Relieved 1/N LANCS...	
2.30 p 27. CUINCHY	Relieved by ¼ 2/YN LANCS Z...	
11.0 p 27.	Relieved 2nd Glosters... Z... (S Walls BUREDEMBERG)	
	Battn HQ Pike Bridge at...	

2nd Infantry Brigade.

1st Division.

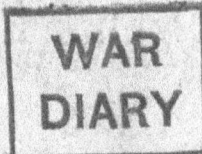

1/9th BATTN. THE KING'S (LIVERPOOL REGIMENT).

J U N E

1 9 1 5

On His Majesty's Service.

WAR DIARY or **INTELLIGENCE SUMMARY.**
(Erase heading not required.)

Army Form C. 2118.

1/9th Batn. "The King's" (Liverpool Regt) T.F.   JUNE 1915

Hour, Date, Place 1915		Summary of Events and Information	Remarks and references to Appendices
3 pm	June 1. ANNEQUIN	Battalion, on arrival by V.N. LANCS (less 1 Company) met by 1 Company 7/R SUSSEX, marched to ANNEQUIN in Brigade Reserve & otherwise normal.	MRC
2 pm	4 LABEUVRIERE	Battalion marched to LABEUVRIERE and not training.	MRC
	11 "	Draft of 75 other ranks arrived from 1/9th Battn. in ENGLAND, 4 other ranks, unders, posted sick to ENGLAND, to join 1/9th Battn.	MRC
10.15 am	16 CUINCHY	Battalion marched via BETHUNE to CUINCHY and relieved 1st COLDSTREAMS in trenches A1.	MRC
	17 "	Casualties: 1 other rank killed.	MRC
	18 "	2 other ranks wounded.	MRC
3.30 pm	19 VERQUIN	Battalion on relief by 1/Royal NORTH LANCS and Subsection A1 marched to VERQUIN. Casualties: 1 other rank killed, 2 wounded.	MRC
10.0	24 LAPUGNOY	Battalion marched to LAPUGNOY. Casualties: 2 other ranks accidentally wounded.	MRC
3.0 pm	27 SAILLY LABOURSE	Battalion marched to SAILLY LABOURSE.	MRC
	30 "	2 O.S. Lieutenants Pryme and B.L.D. Lewis for duty.	MRC

E.J. Ramsay Lieut. Col.
Commanding, 1/9th BATT. "THE KING'S."

2nd Infantry Brigade.
1st Division.

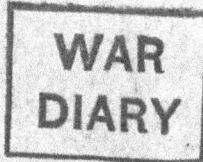

1/9th BATTN. THE KING'S (LIVERPOOL REGIMENT).

J U L Y

1 9 1 5

On His Majesty's Service.

WAR DIARY
or
INTELLIGENCE SUMMARY.

Army Form C. 2118.

(Erase heading not required.)

War Diary of the King's (Liverpool R.(T.F.) Bn.) T.F. July 1915.

Instructions regarding War Diaries and Intelligence Summaries are contained in F.S. Regs., Part II. and the Staff Manual respectively. Title pages will be prepared in manuscript.

Hour, Date, Place 1915		Summary of Events and Information	Remarks and references to Appendices
2 pm July 2	CAMBRIN	Battalion left SAILLY LABOURSE and relieved 2R/SUSSEX in Z.2 S.N. sector of Trenches.	
4	"	1 other rank wounded.	
6	"	1 Officer (2nd Lieut. E.L. CHESTER) killed, 1 other rank wounded	
5 pm 7	SAILLY LABOURSE	Battalion was relieved by 5R/SUSSEX and 1 Company 2R/SUSSEX, marched to SAILLY LABOURSE. In Brigade Reserve.	
9		Fighting Strength 20 officers 797 other Ranks.	
6 pm 12	FAUBOURG D'ARRAS BETHUNE	Battalion marched to BETHUNE, in Divisional Reserve	
8 pm 19	LABOURSE	Battalion marched to LABOURSE. in Brigade Reserve	
21	"	Lieut J.H. HALLIWELL reported for duty from 7/9th Bn ENGLAND	
24		2 other ranks wounded	
5 pm 25	VERMELLES	Battalion marched to VERMELLES and relieved 5R/SUSSEX in Y.2.	
28		Lieut W.G.B. EDWARDS arrived for duty from 7/9th Bn ENGLAND	
30		3 other ranks wounded, 1 other rank died of wounds	
11.45 pm 31	FAUBOURG D'ARRAS BETHUNE	Battalion, relieved by 2/R MUNSTER FUSILIERS, marched to BETHUNE	

E. Munson Lieut. Col.
Commanding, 1/5th Bn. "THE KING'S."

2nd Infantry Brigade.
1st Division.

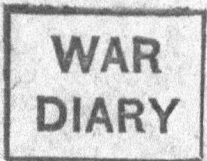

1/9th BATTN. THE KING'S (LIVERPOOL REGIMENT).

A U G U S T

1 9 1 5

On His Majesty's Service.

Army Form C. 2118.

WAR DIARY
or
INTELLIGENCE SUMMARY.
(Erase heading not required.)

1/9th Battalion THE KINGS
(Liverpool Regt.) T.F.
August 1915

Hour, Date, Place			Summary of Events and Information	Remarks and references to Appendices
1915				
Aug	3	FAUBOURG BARAKS BETHUNE	*[illegible entry]*	M.C.
2 pm	6		The Battalion marched to ANNEQUIN and took over billets from 1st CAMERON HIGHLANDERS, 2 Brigade Reserve Troops	M.C.
	7/10	ANNEQUIN	*[illegible]*	M.C.
	10	"	The Battalion took over FACTORY TRENCH from LANCASHIRE FUSILIERS	M.C.
	12	"	The Battalion relieved by 2/ROYAL SUSSEX in FACTORY TRENCH	M.C.
3 pm	14	"	*[illegible]*	M.C.
	15		*[illegible]*	M.C.
6 pm	16	LABOURSE	The Battalion relieved by 2/ROYAL SUSSEX in Z1, and marched to LABOURSE in Brigade Reserve	M.C.
1.30 pm	18	GARDEN CITY	The Battalion moved to GARDEN CITY — Machine Gun Section ANNEQUIN moved to "Z" trench as Brigade Reserve	M.C.
	20		*[illegible]*	M.C.
1.45 pm	23	ANNEQUIN	*[illegible]* Brig. General G.F. THESIGER C.B. C.M.G. — PERONNE	M.C.
	24		The Battalion relieved and marched to FOUQUIERES, VERQUIN, VERQUINGHUL, LABOURSE, SAILLY LABOURSE and ANNEQUIN, relieving 1ST CAMERON HIGHLANDERS in Y4 and YK	M.C.
	25		Four Officers Lt. EASHTON, Lt. LAWRENCE, Mr. MANSERGH	M.C.
	26			
	27			
	28	NOYELLES-LES-VERMELLES	The Battalion was relieved by 1/LOYAL NORTH LANCS.	M.C.
	29		Lieut R.S. WOODWARD and Lieut RANGELES went to "B" & "D". Lieut F. ATKINSON, 2/Lts. "A" & "D". "THE KINGS" joined for duty	M.C.
	30		Lieut C.H.W.L. BROWN attached H.Q. Covert. Lt. R. (?) & C. "THE KINGS" joined for duty	M.C.
	31		*[illegible]*	M.C.

Commanding 1/9th Batt. "THE KINGS"
Lieut. Col.
[signature]

2nd Infantry Brigade.
1st Division.

WAR DIARY

1/9th BATTN. THE KING'S (LIVERPOOL REGIMENT).

S E P T E M B E R

1 9 1 5

WAR DIARY or INTELLIGENCE SUMMARY

Army Form C. 2118.

(Erase heading not required.)

Hour, Date, Place	Summary of Events and Information	Remarks and references to Appendices
Sept. 1 NOYELLES	Engaged in clearing up & establishing Billets. 1st & 2nd advance guards of Batt. arrived to Battn. Strictly advance of Col: Mackenzie	
2		
3	Batt. moved to GARDEN CITY	
	Batt. moved to BURBURE — Draft of 30 N.C.O's & men from 3rd Entrenching Batt. joined for duty	
17 BURBURE	20 N.C.O's & men from 3rd Entrenching Batt. joined for duty	
10	Batt. moved to LAPUGNOY into billets	
13	Batt. moved to VERQUIN into billets	
14	Batt. moved to Vincles and took up position in Y1	
25/26	Batt. took part in attack on German line — captured 3-400 prisoners. Casualties 11 officers 223 other ranks	
	Batt. moved to MAZINGARBE into billets — Capt & QM Stoker & Major Lewis joined for duty — moved to Noeulles in S.E. corner of LOOS	
28	Draft of 60 N.C.O's and men from 3rd Entrenching Batt. joined for duty	
29	Draft of 30 N.C.O's & men from Base joined for duty — took over Beachers by Bn. Batt. Entrenched	
30		

H. B. [signature] Lieut. Col.
Commanding, 1/9th BATT. "THE KING'S."

2nd Infantry Brigade.

1st Division.

(Left Bde. to join 3rd
Bde. 12.11.15).

WAR DIARY

1/9th BATTN. THE KING'S (LIVERPOOL REGIMENT).

O C T O B E R

1 9 1 5

On His Majesty's Service.

Army Form C. 2118

WAR DIARY
or
INTELLIGENCE SUMMARY.
(Erase heading not required.)

Instructions regarding War Diaries and Intelligence Summaries are contained in F. S. Regs., Part II. and the Staff Manual respectively. Title pages will be prepared in manuscript.

Hour, Date, Place	Summary of Events and Information	Remarks and references to Appendices
Oct 1/15	Ruth returned explains how South East of town 3 others wounded	
" 3	Took over trench on NOEUX-LES-MINES - Batn refitted	
" 6		
" 7	Mines to MAZINGARBE and took over trench	
" 8	Took over a portion of the line on North East side of LOOS Brought up after 4.15 Enemy opened a violent artillery and machine gun fire from 5 hours a heavy machine gun and rifle fire also sustained	
11AM		
4/1/4	Every chance to attack on our lives strongly supported Attack repulsed with severe loss to the enemy Our Capable, 1 Officer killed & wounded and 28 others who heart and wounded We still had 6 galtrative reserves from Division and Brigade on event of the got	
" 9		
" 10	further exploitation from 10th Capt, 1st Army south of the 8th	
" 13	your hilles and 3 other ricks wounded	
" 14/15	Released from line and proceed to NOEUX-LES-MINES and entrained for LILLERS where to be went into rest	

H. Ramsay Lieut. Col.
Commanding, 1/9th BATT. "THE KING'S"

1ST DIVISION
3RD BRIGADE

1-9TH BATTALION

THE KING'S (LIVERPOOL REGT.)

NOV - DEC 1915

3rd Infantry Brigade.

1st Division.

(Joined Bde. from 2nd Bde. 1st Div. 12.11.15.)

WAR DIARY

1/9th BATTN. THE KING'S (LIVERPOOL REGIMENT).

NOVEMBER

1915

On His Majesty's Service.

WAR DIARY

9th Bn. The King's (Liverpool Regt.)

Army Form C. 2118.

INTELLIGENCE SUMMARY.

(Erase heading not required.)

Hour, Date, Place		Summary of Events and Information	Remarks and references to Appendices
1915 November	1 LILLERS	Battalion at rest in LILLERS. Training.	MAPS:—
	3 "	Draft of 90 N.C.O. and men joined battalion from 3/9th battalion for duty.	BETHUNE, Contains 36A S.E, 36 S.W. Sheet 36B N.E, 36G N.W. Scale 1/40,000
	5 "	2nd Lt. F.B. LEBELL appointed Battalion Scout officer.	
	6 "	Lieut E. PAYNE and 17 other ranks went to TERFAY CHATEAU for course of instruction in trench mortars	
	7 "	Company Serjeant Major P.? Byrne awarded MEDAILLE MILITAIRE	
	15 "	Two other ranks went to TERFAY CHATEAU for course of instruction in use of trench mortars.	TRENCH MAP 36C N.W. 3. adjusted 1/12 acres Provisional Edition No 3 Scale 1/10,000
8:45 p.m. 15 "		Battalion marched to billets in HOUCHIN Training continued.	
10:30 a.m. 19 HOUCHIN		Battalion marched to billets in PHILOSOPHE. Began work of clearing out and reorganising billeting area that road making &c.	
21 PHILOSOPHE		2nd Lieuts R DARLING and W RAINE joined battalion for duty.	
22 "		2nd Lieutenant L.L.S. RICHER reported for duty with battalion. Draft of 46 other ranks reported for duty with battalion.	
23 "		Lieut H.W. NEWTON and 17 other ranks went to TERFAY CHATEAU for course of instruction in trenching.	

WAR DIARY
or
INTELLIGENCE SUMMARY.
(Erase heading not required.)

9th Bn. The King's
(Liverpool Regt.)

Army Form C. 2118.

Hour, Date, Place	Summary of Events and Information	Remarks and references to Appendices
1915		MAPS:-
November 23 PHILOSOPHE	Lt PAYNE and 17 other ranks returned from Iondaigues.	BETHUNE
5.30pm - 26 -	Battalion marched out and reported part time trenches along west side of road from H25 a 87 to H19 c 79. The 1st Bn GLOUCESTERSHIRE REGT was on our right and the 2nd Bn. ROYAL BERKSHIRE REGT on our left. Snow lying on ground. One man killed by snipers and three wounded by shell fire. Freezing.	Contoned Sheet { 36A SE, 36S W, 36D NE, 36C NW Scale 1/40,000
- 28 Between LOOS and HULLUCH	One man wounded by shell fire. During the night battalion was relieved by 2nd Bn. WELCH REGT and moved to reserve trenches in old German front line in G23 A. Mud very deep in trenches causing all movement to be extremely slow and difficult.	TRENCH MAP 36c N.W. 3 and pts of 1, 2 and 4 Provisional Edition No. 3 Scale 1/10,000
- 29 -		
- 30 G23 a	Remained in reserve trenches	

3rd Infantry Brigade.
1st Division.

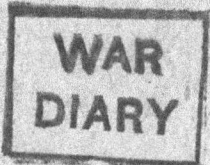

1/9th BATTN. THE KING'S (LIVERPOOL REGIMENT).

DECEMBER

1915

On His Majesty's Service.

WAR DIARY
INTELLIGENCE SUMMARY

9th Battalion THE KING'S (LIVERPOOL REGIMENT)

Army Form C. 2118.

Hour, Date, Place	Summary of Events and Information	Remarks and references to Appendices
1915		TRENCH MAP
December 1 G 23	In reserve trenches. Four other ranks wounded	36C N.W.3
2 7pm	Marched to billets in NOEUX LES MINES in K.18. eovs	East and partly 1, 2 and 4
3 NOEUX LES MINES	Training. Improvement of billetting area eovs	are
4	— — 2nd Lieut RICHER returned from leave eovs	BETHUNE COMBINED SHEET
5	Rest. 2nd Lieut DARLING and 2nd Lieut RAINE returned from leave eovs	
6	Training. Improvement of billetting area eovs	
7	— —	
8 3pm	Left billets and marched through MAZINGARBE to reserve trenches in Q.17 B and D eovs	
9 Q.17 B & D	Improvement of trenches and making of shelter for troops eovs. 2nd Lieut ASHTON went on leave eovs. 2nd Lieut ATKINSON returned from leave eovs. One man wounded.	
10	Same as 9th.	
11 6pm	Same as 9th.	
12 H.19A & G.19B	Took over front line trenches H19A08 to G1838 6 from 6th WELCH, 2nd ROYAL SUSSEX on right — 1st GLOUCESTERS on left. eovs	
13	Weather wet and cold. Enemy fairly quiet eovs. Same as 12th. One man wounded. eovs	

Army Form C. 2118.

WAR DIARY
or
INTELLIGENCE SUMMARY.   9th Battalion THE KING'S (LIVERPOOL REGIMENT)

(Erase heading not required.)

Instructions regarding War Diaries and Intelligence Summaries are contained in F.S. Regs., Part II. and the Staff Manual respectively. Title pages will be prepared in manuscript.

Hour, Date, Place	Summary of Events and Information	Remarks and references to Appendices
1915		
December 14 H.19.A & G.18.B		
9 p.m. 15 G.17.B and D	Relieved by 6th WELCH and returned to reserve trenches i. G.17.B & D. Improvement of trenches and making of new support trench.	
16	Same as 15th. 2nd Lieut LEBELL went on leave.	
17 6 p.m.	Took over front line trenches H.19.A.0.8 & G.13.B.86 from 6th WELCH. LONDON SCOTTISH on right – 1st GLOUCESTERS on left.	
18 G.13.B & H.31	Improvement of trenches and making of new support trench. 2nd Lieut ASHTON returned from leave.	
19	Same as 18th. Captain WOODERSON R.A.M.C. attached, went on leave, being relieved by Lieut McFARLAND R.A.M.C.	
20 7 p.m.	Relieved by 5th KING'S OWN ROYAL LANCASTERS and marched to billets i. MAZINGARBE.	
21 MAZINGARBE	Cleaning up. Large carrying parties at night. Draft of 26 other ranks joined unit.	
22	Training and fatigues.	
23	Same as 22nd. 2nd Lieut MANSERGH went on leave.	
24	Same as 22nd. 2nd Lieut LEBELL returned from leave.	

Army Form C. 2118.

WAR DIARY
INTELLIGENCE SUMMARY. 9th Battalion THE KING'S
(LIVERPOOL REGIMENT)

(Erase heading not required.)

Instructions regarding War Diaries and Intelligence Summaries are contained in F.S. Regs., Part II. and the Staff Manual respectively. Title pages will be prepared in manuscript.

Hour, Date, Place	Summary of Events and Information	Remarks and references to Appendices
1915		
December 25 MAZINGARBE	Rest. 2015.	
26 2.30 p.m.	Left billets and marched to front line trenches H25A85 to H19A08. Took over from LONDON SCOTTISH - 2nd WELCH on right - 2nd ROYAL SUSSEX on left. One man wounded - 2nd Lt ROBERTS attached to Brigade Pioneers 2015	
27. H25A - H19A	Trenches in bad state - men very wet - mud - work done in repairing and draining. 2015	
28	Same as 27th. One man wounded. 2015	
29 8 p.m.	Relieved by 6th WELCH and moved to Reserve Trenches in G23	
30 G23 + G24	Work done on improvement of Reserve Trench & Communication Trenches and construction of NORTHERN SAP REDOUBT about G22 B97. 2015	
31	Same as 30th. Lieut DIGGORY and one other rank wounded during bombardment of Reserve Trench in G24. 2015	

www.ingramcontent.com/pod-product-compliance
Lightning Source LLC
Chambersburg PA
CBHW081459160426
43193CB00013B/2541